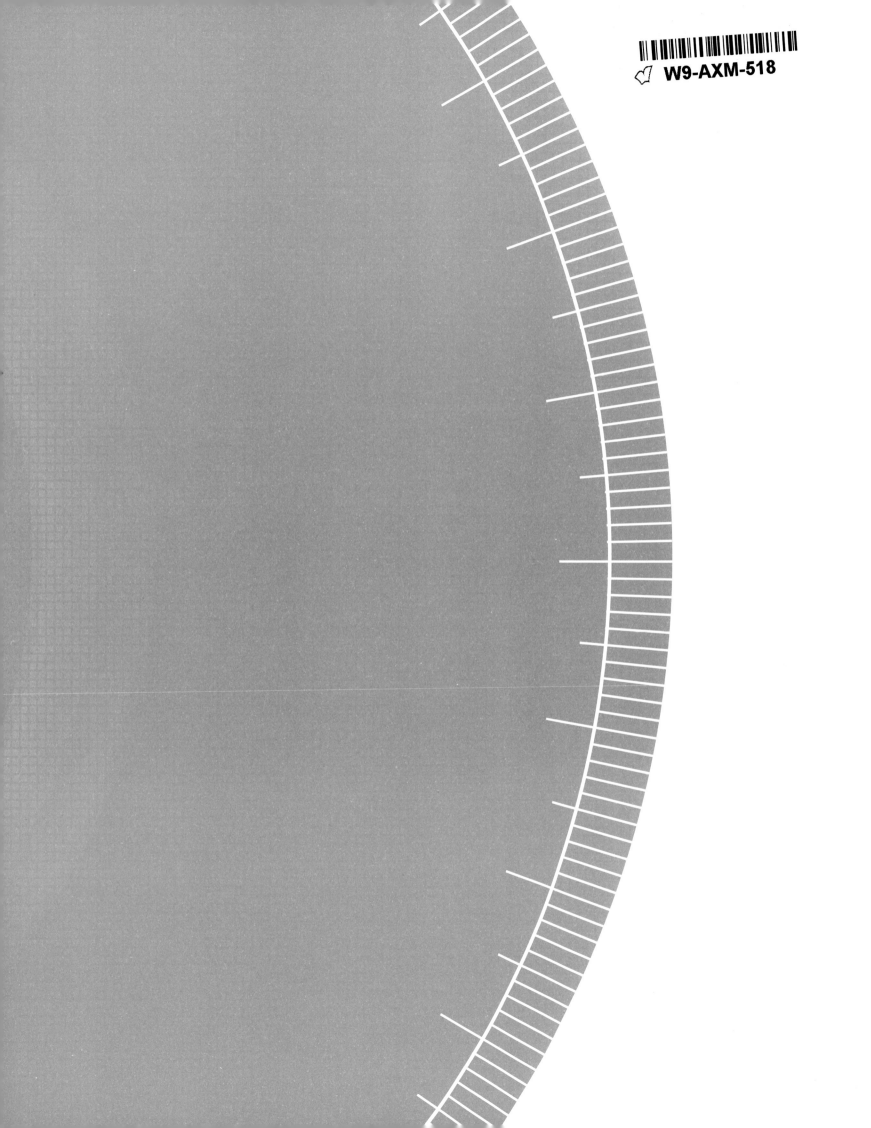

CONSULTANT
Richard Walker

# THE HUMAN BODY IN 360°

explored in 5 virtual journeys

Digestion

Breathing

Circulation

Hearing

New Life

CARLTON KIDS

Published in 2012 by Carlton Books Limited,
an imprint of the Carlton Publishing Group,
20 Mortimer Street, London W1T 3JW

2 4 6 8 10 9 7 5 3 1

**Original concept:** Victoria Marshallsay
**Project Editor:** Victoria Marshallsay
**Written by:** Salima Hirani and Richard Walker
**Art Directors:** Russell Porter and Clare Baggaley
**Designer:** Ceri Hurst
**Picture Research:** Ben White
**QTVR imaging:** Adam Questell
**Production**: Christine Ni

My name is MEL
(Mechanical Exploration Leader)

We are going on these amazing
voyages together. I can't wait to
find out what happens to the food
I eat, the air I breathe and how
I can hear! Let's go.

# CONTENTS

# HOW TO START YOUR ADVENTURE

Using the wonders of QTVR (*Quick Time Virtual Reality*) on the enclosed CD, you will be taken on **5 journeys inside a virtual body**. The book will give you a guided tour of what you are seeing and more.

## Let the adventure begin.

## What do I need?

To start your voyages you will need a PC or Macintosh computer that meets the minimum system requirements which are:

- An optical drive (CD/DVD)

- A suitable web browser, such as Internet Explorer, Firefox, Chrome, or Safari

**You do not need to be connected to the Internet to use this CD.**

## What is QTVR?

QTVR (Quick Time Virtual Reality) is 360° panoramic photography. With QTVR you can travel though time and space and you can zoom in to see something more closely. Using QTVR here you can explore vital journeys that take place in your body and look at the key organs.

# This is what you have to do

- Insert *The Human Body in 360°* CD into your computer
- Find the folder named **The Human Body in 360°** on the DVD
- Copy this folder on to your desktop or to a hard drive
- Remove the CD
- To launch your virtual journeys, open the folder on your computer and double-click on **The Human Body in 360°** and then the journey you would like to start with.
- Click on the journey you have chosen. You will be taken to the first **camera hotspot**.

# What is a camera hotspot?

This is the position of the camera inside the virtual body.

For example, if you begin with *Hearing and the journey of sound*, the first **camera hotspot** is in the ear canal. From here you can see towards the outside world one way and the eardrum the other way.

Using your mouse you can take a 360° tour of this part of the ear. If you look towards the inside of the ear and the eardrum you will see a **blue icon**. If you click on this you will be taken to the next camera hotspot in the middle ear — the next part in the journey of sound.

JOURNEY

**1**

DIGESTION

Follow the food!

## Why do you eat?

### You eat because you are hungry, but what is hunger?

It's your body reporting that it's low on the supplies needed for building and maintaining cells. And you can't just send an apple or a slice of pie straight into your bloodstream. Food has to be broken down by the **digestive system**.

This happens as food passes down a long tube called your **digestive tract**. Different parts of this tube have their own job to do, starting at the **mouth** and **throat** and going all the way down to the **anus**, from which waste products are expelled. In between, the food travels amazingly long distances around your **stomach**, **small intestine** and **large intestine**, all of which extract as much goodness from it as possible.

Food comes in thousands of different varieties, but it all breaks down into a small number of substances that are useful to your body. This chapter explains how!

★ Insert the CD into your CD drive.
★ Pick your journey and follow the QTVR symbols.
★ Let the adventure begin!

# DIGESTION
## Follow the food!

The camera is positioned in four places along the digestive tract: in your mouth, at the entrance of your throat, inside your stomach and in your small intestine. The CD takes you on the same route as a piece of food that you begin chewing in your mouth. The following pages explain the vital parts and what's happening along the way.

## YOU ARE IN THE MOUTH

You can see your tongue, your teeth, the sides and roof of your mouth, and the back of your throat.

It's a long way down there.

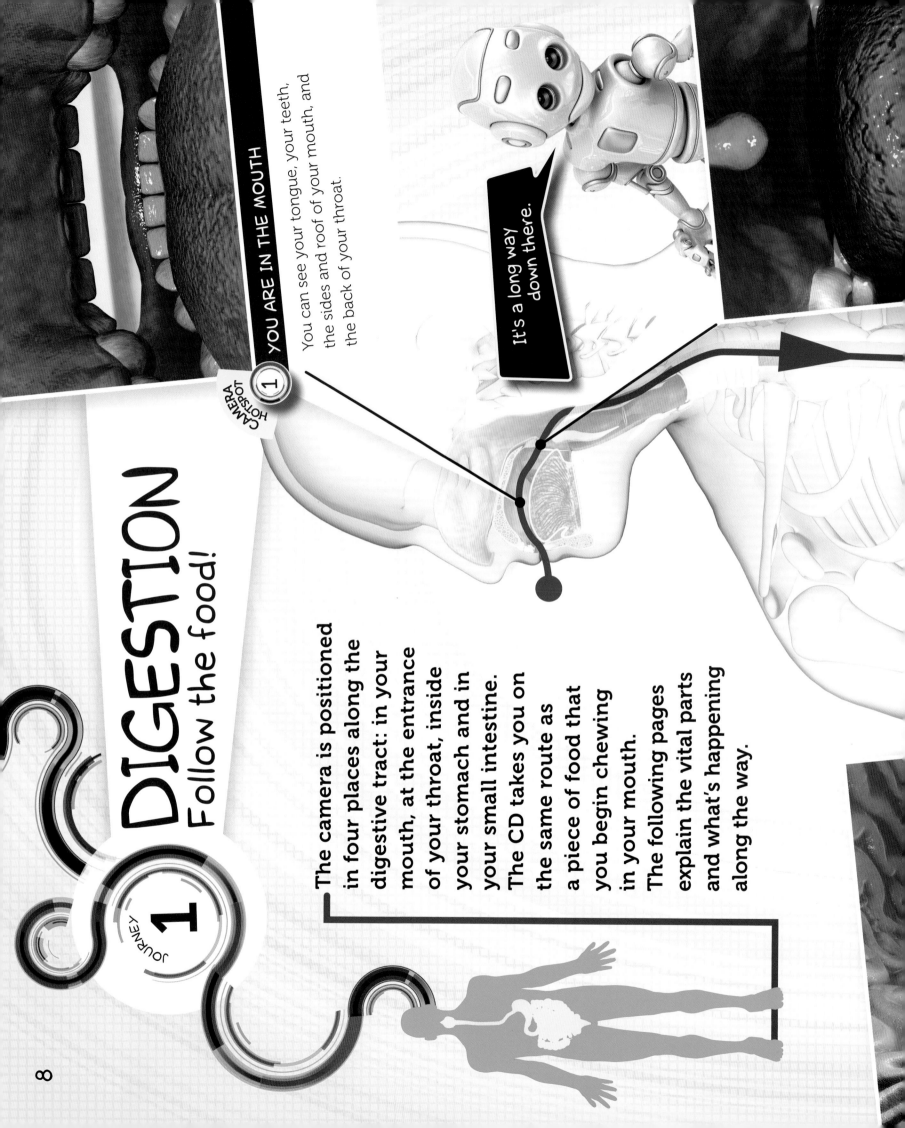

## ② YOU ARE AT THE BACK OF THE THROAT

Look up to your nasal cavity, forwards into your mouth and down to the epiglottis and the opening of the oesophagus behind your vocal cords.

## ③ YOU ARE INSIDE THE STOMACH

You can see the strong walls of your stomach. If you look to the right you can see the entrance from the oesophagus and to the left, the exit to your small intestine. These are explained on pages 12–13.

## ④ YOU ARE INSIDE THE SMALL INTESTINE

This is the longest part of the digestive tract and where the nutrients from food pass into your blood. Learn more about this on page 13.

# Your mouth and throat

Do you chew your food properly? If not, you're creating extra work for your stomach, as it has to break down great big lumps of food! Your body cannot obtain energy from food until it is chopped up and digested, which releases the nutrients in the food in a form that the body can use.

## Your mouth

During an average lifetime a person will eat 20 tonnes of food. That's the same as the weight of four bull elephants. Whatever you eat is hacked into small pieces and mashed by your teeth with the help of saliva and your tongue. Once the food has been transformed into a form that can be swallowed, the tongue moves it towards the **throat** for swallowing. The **lips** close to hold the food in the mouth as it works and the **cheeks** expand outwards. Without the work done by the mouth, you'd continually be getting solid chips or whole strawberries stuck in your throat!

FOOD

PERISTALSIS

## What happens when I swallow?

As soon as food touches your throat a reflex action is triggered and a flap of cartilage called the epiglottis closes over the entrance to the trachea (windpipe) to stop you choking. Food passes this as it is pushed into the oesophagus. Muscles in your oesophagus begin a series of wave-like contractions, called peristalsis, which push the food towards the stomach. This part of the journey is pretty quick – it only takes about 10 seconds.

## SALIVARY GLANDS

Your mouth has three pairs of salivary glands that release slimy spit or saliva. There are two glands beneath the tongue, and one gland in front of the ear. Saliva is mixed with food to begin digestion.

## THROAT

When food is swallowed it enters your throat, which pushes it to the top of your oesophagus.

## EPIGLOTTIS

This flap of cartilage behind your tongue moves down to cover the entrance to your trachea when swallowing, so that food does not enter the trachea or lungs.

## TEETH

Adult humans normally have 32 teeth. There are different types of teeth that prepare food for swallowing in a variety of ways. Incisors (most people have eight) act like knives, slicing up the food; canines (four) grasp and pierce it; premolars (eight) and molars (12) grind up and crush it.

## TONGUE

This muscular, flexible organ has a rough surface allowing it to grip the food as it moves around your mouth. Your tongue is also covered with taste buds that allow you to taste the food you are eating, increasing your enjoyment of it or helping you to detect a substance that is poisonous.

## Why am I sick?

Sometimes, your body needs to press the ejector button to get food out of your body. Muscles in the wall of your abdomen squeeze the stomach and reverse peristalsis pushes the food up the oesophagus and out of the mouth with force. This self-protection mechanism gets rid of food that has gone off or is poisonous, helping the body fight damage and disease. It also makes a horrible mess!

## OESOPHAGUS

This muscular tube connects your throat to your stomach. Its lining releases slimy, slippery mucus that enables swallowed food to slide smoothly down to your stomach.

# Your stomach and guts

After being swallowed, the next stop for food is the stomach where the main work of digestion begins. It can take about 24–36 hours, depending on how much you have eaten and the type of food it is. In that time, food travels along the intestines, which are looped over many times in order to fit their length inside your body.

## How does food become poo?

Your **stomach** continues the work started by your mouth, and breaks down food by churning it into small particles. The gloopy substance that results is then passed into the **small intestine**. Ignore the name – this is the largest part of the digestive tract. It can be up to 7m long, which is nearly the length of a bus!

In the stomach and small intestine, food is broken down into simple nutrients by chemicals called enzymes. Anything remaining travels to the **large intestine**, where undigestible leftovers are compressed into poo (faeces). At the end of the intestine is the **anus**, where the faeces exit the body when you go to the toilet. It all looks very different by that point, but most things that come out originally came in through your mouth!

### Why does my stomach rumble?

This normally happens when you are hungry and your stomach contains just some liquid and air. Your brain sends hunger signals to your stomach so it starts to contract. This squeezes the gas inside the stomach and ... *GROWWWWLL!*

**GALL BLADDER**

This releases bile, which helps digest fats in the food you eat.

**DUODENUM**

This is the first section of your small intestine.

**PANCREAS**

This releases pancreatic juice along a tube into the duodenum. It contains enzymes that digest carbohydrates, fats and proteins.

**LARGE INTESTINE**

The parts of the food you eat that cannot be digested by the small intestine are passed along the digestive tract into the large intestine, where any useful substances (such as salts and water) are extracted from them. As the waste products continue along the tract, they become semi-solid faeces that are held in your rectum until they can be pushed out through your anus, the opening at the far end of the tract.

**RECTUM**

**ANUS**

## LIVER

This is your body's larder. It stores vitamins, minerals and sugars for your body to use as required, and transforms some nutrients into other, more useful forms. It also converts harmful substances (such as alcohol) into safer ones.

## STOMACH

This stretchy bag is large enough to accommodate up to 2 litres, so it can hold an entire meal in one go. Its muscular walls contract to stretch it in different directions, which squeezes and pulverises the food within it. Glands in your stomach's lining release enzymes that digest proteins. After spending a few hours in your stomach, the chewed-up food is transformed into a mushy liquid, which slowly oozes into the small intestine.

## SMALL INTESTINE

The lining of your small intestine releases more enzymes to break down the mushy food into even smaller pieces, until it is completely broken down and digested. By now, the food has been converted into molecules that are small enough to pass through the lining of your small intestine into the blood that flows through the lining. The molecules are carried to other parts of your body in the bloodstream to supply energy. Most of them end up in your liver, which stores and processes them.

## VILLI

The lining of your small intestine is covered with tiny finger-like villi, which give it a much larger surface area than it would have if it were flat. In fact, the surface area is roughly equivalent to the size of a football pitch. These villi absorb the digested food molecules. Inside each villus are capillaries or blood vessels into which the molecules pass. From here, they travel around the body in the bloodstream to wherever they are needed. Each villus also has a tube (lacteals) containing lymph, another body fluid that carries fat away.

VILLUS COVERING IS ONE CELL THICK

CAPILLARY NETWORK

LACTEAL

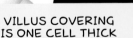

# JOURNEY

# 2

# BREATHING

Take a trip in the air!

## Why do we need air?

**Oxygen is an invisible gas that makes up one-fifth of the air.**

It's vital to all living things, and helps them to extract energy from foods such as sugar. That energy then keeps your cells alive.

Everyone needs oxygen to survive, and you get it by breathing fresh air into your lungs, absorbing some of the oxygen from it, and breathing out stale air afterwards. This process is called ventilation. Air is breathed into the body via the **nose** and sometimes the **mouth**. It travels down the **throat**, larynx (voice box), trachea (windpipe) to the **lungs** and into the **blood**. It might be invisible, but oxygen is as vital to your body as water.

★ Insert your DVD into your CD drive.
★ Pick your journey and follow the QTVR symbols.
★ Let the adventure begin!

# BREATHING
## Take a trip in the air!

The camera is positioned in six places: in your nasal cavity, behind your nose at the top of your throat, at the back of your throat, inside your trachea, inside a bronchiole and inside an alveolus. The DVD takes you on the same route as the air you breathe. The following pages explain the vital parts and what is happening along the way.

**CAMERA HOTSPOT 1 — YOU ARE INSIDE THE NASAL CAVITY**

If you look down you can see out of the nostril to the outside world. Look the other way and you can see the nasal structures that warm and moisten air.

**CAMERA HOTSPOT 2 — YOU ARE AT THE TOP OF THE THROAT**

You can see the back view of the structures within your nasal cavity. If you look down you can see your epiglottis and vocal cords.

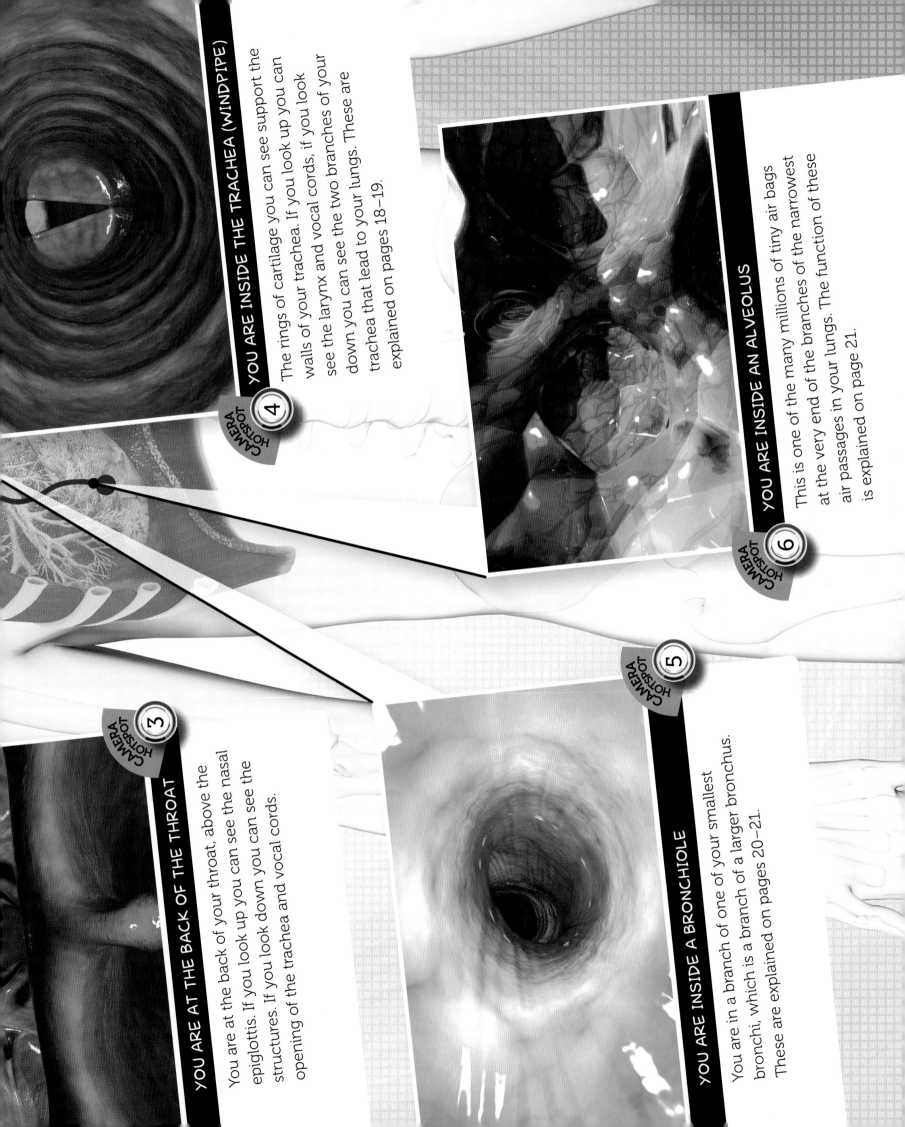

## YOU ARE INSIDE THE TRACHEA (WINDPIPE)

The rings of cartilage you can see support the walls of your trachea. If you look up you can see the larynx and vocal cords, if you look down you can see the two branches of your trachea that lead to your lungs. These are explained on pages 18–19.

**CAMERA HOTSPOT 4**

## YOU ARE INSIDE AN ALVEOLUS

This is one of the many millions of tiny air bags at the very end of the branches of the narrowest air passages in your lungs. The function of these is explained on page 21.

**CAMERA HOTSPOT 6**

**CAMERA HOTSPOT 5**

## YOU ARE AT THE BACK OF THE THROAT

You are at the back of your throat, above the epiglottis. If you look up you can see the nasal structures. If you look down you can see the opening of the trachea and vocal cords.

**CAMERA HOTSPOT 3**

## YOU ARE INSIDE A BRONCHIOLE

You are in a branch of one of your smallest bronchi, which is a branch of a larger bronchus. These are explained on pages 20–21.

# Breathing in and out

The average person at rest breathes in and out about 10–14 times per minute. After great activity, such as running, your breathing rate may increase to 50–60 times each minute. Air is breathed in and out through your nose and mouth and travels down to the lungs where oxygen passes into your blood to be delivered to your body's cells.

## Take a deep breath

Once you've breathed in, air is filtered to remove dust and dirt, then warmed up for the lungs to deal with comfortably. The nasal cavity, throat, larynx (voice box) and trachea (windpipe) help with these important tasks.

### NOSTRILS

Air is breathed in through these two openings that are guarded by dirt-filtering hairs.

### NASAL CAVITY

Air is warmed, moistened and cleaned as it swirls through the space behind the nostrils.

## Bless you!

When tiny bits of dirt make your nose tickle, your body takes a deep breath and closes your vocal cords. When they open again, air blasts out at up to 160kph.

As the air shoots through your nostrils, it takes with it germs and beads of mucus to clear your nose. That's why it's important to sneeze into a tissue, and avoid spreading infection around.

### TRACHEA (WINDPIPE)

Air passes along it, going to and from your lungs. Its walls are reinforced by tough, c-shaped rings of cartilage, making it strong and sturdy, and are lined with mucus in order to trap any fine particles of dust and dirt that have made it this far into your body. The lining of your trachea is covered with tiny hair-like filaments known as cilia, which transport dirt-laden mucus back up to your throat so that it can be swallowed. Acid in your stomach destroys any debris or bacteria that the mucus has picked up and trapped.

## MOUTH

Usually, air is breathed in through your nostrils, but your mouth can also breathe in air, which is very useful during exercise or if you have a blocked nose.

## THROAT

Also known as the pharynx, this tube connects your nasal cavity to your voice box.

## EPIGLOTTIS

This flap covers the entrance to your trachea so that food doesn't make its way into your lungs when you swallow.

## LARYNX (VOICE BOX)

This tube connects your throat to your trachea. When you speak, it is your larynx that makes the sounds.

## VOCAL CORDS

These two membranes are stretched across your larynx and contain muscles that pull them together or apart to produce sound.

## How do I produce sound?

**Being able to use language makes humans very special in the animal kingdom,** and your vocal cords are a vital part of the process. These two stiff membranes are stretched across your larynx, which contains muscles that pull them together or apart. When you're breathing normally, the two membranes are far apart so air can pass through.

When you want to talk, the muscles pull the membranes nearer together so the gap between them is closed or very narrow. Bursts of air from your lungs pass between them to produce sound vibrations which are shaped into speech by your tongue and lips. Try to speak and swallow at the same time – it's impossible!

## CORDS CLOSED

Your vocal cords are drawn together and pulled taut for sound-making.

## CORDS OPEN

Looking down along the throat, you can see your vocal cords are drawn apart, allowing you to breathe normally. You can also see the c-shaped rings of the trachea beyond the larynx.

# Where does air go?

From your trachea (windpipe), breathed-in air travels to your lungs, which are made up of bronchi, bronchioles and alveoli. Your lungs do the vital work of taking oxygen into your bloodstream and removing the waste product carbon dioxide. This is made when your cells use oxygen to release energy from food.

## A tree-like system

**Your lungs are two large spongy organs filled with air passages.** They are located in your **chest cavity**, at the bottom of your **trachea (windpipe)**.

Your trachea splits into two branches, the left and right bronchi. These divide into smaller bronchi and even smaller bronchioles. Together your trachea, bronchi and bronchiole resemble an upside-down tree.

At the tips of each of the smallest bronchioles are small air bags called **alveoli** through which oxygen passes into your bloodstream. Your bloodstream drops off carbon dioxide at the alveoli so it can be breathed out. Breathing out carbon dioxide is just as important as breathing in oxygen, as carbon dioxide is poisonous in large amounts.

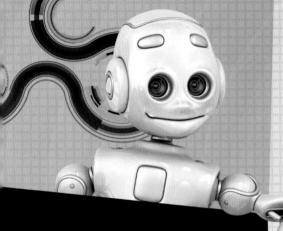

## THE DIAPHRAGM

Your diaphragm separates your chest from your abdomen. This dome-shaped muscle, along with the muscles between your ribs, enables your lungs to expand and shrink during breathing.

### INTERCOSTAL MUSCLE

The muscles between your ribs pull your ribcage up when you breathe in.

### RIGHT LUNG

This is larger than your left lung.

### RIB

Your ribcage, which consists of 24 curved bones, provides your heart and lungs with protection against blows to your body – like armour.

### BRONCHIOLE

The smallest of your bronchi branch into very tiny air passages known as bronchioles.

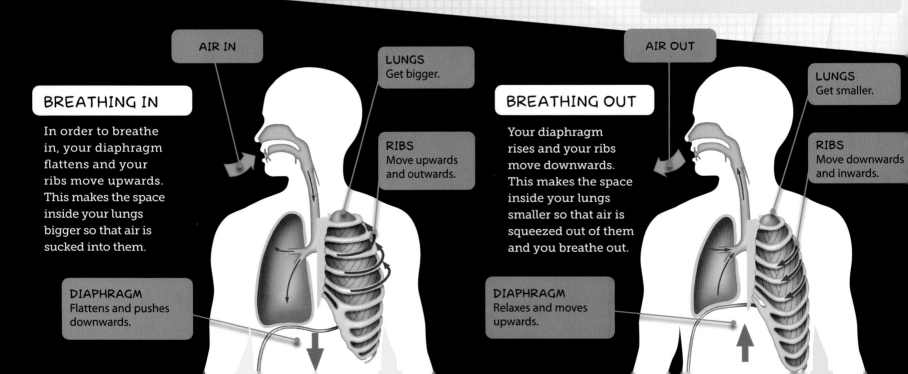

**AIR IN**

**LUNGS**
Get bigger.

## BREATHING IN

In order to breathe in, your diaphragm flattens and your ribs move upwards. This makes the space inside your lungs bigger so that air is sucked into them.

**RIBS**
Move upwards and outwards.

**DIAPHRAGM**
Flattens and pushes downwards.

**AIR OUT**

**LUNGS**
Get smaller.

## BREATHING OUT

Your diaphragm rises and your ribs move downwards. This makes the space inside your lungs smaller so that air is squeezed out of them and you breathe out.

**RIBS**
Move downwards and inwards.

**DIAPHRAGM**
Relaxes and moves upwards.

# What are alveoli?

They are tiny air bags in your lungs. You have over 300 million of them in your chest, which are arranged in bunches at the ends of your narrowest air passages. Each bunch is surrounded by lots of tiny blood vessels that bring in oxygen-poor blood and carry it away again, filled with oxygen.

The distance between the inside of the alveolus and the inside of a capillary is incredibly small, which makes it very quick and easy for oxygen and carbon dioxide to pass through.

In total, the surface area of your alveoli is roughly equivalent to a tennis court, but is packed into the chest in a space no larger than a shopping bag!

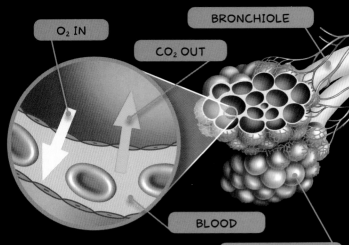

$O_2$ IN

$CO_2$ OUT

BRONCHIOLE

BLOOD

ALVEOLUS

TRACHEA

## LEFT LUNG

This is smaller than your right lung, because it has to make space for your heart, which is situated towards your body's left side. Because your lungs are close to your heart, blood has to travel only a short distance from your heart to pick up oxygen from your lungs.

## BRONCHUS

When your trachea branches off into two smaller air passages, each branch is known as a bronchus. These, in turn, divide into smaller bronchi and then bronchioles.

BRONCHI

## HEART

Your heart pumps blood low in oxygen to the lungs, which refresh it. The newly oxygen-rich blood is then pumped to all your body's cells.

## DIAPHRAGM

This large sheet of muscle is located below your lungs and plays an important role in breathing in and out.

21

## What does my heart do?

**Your heart
constantly pumps
blood around your body
to supply its needs.**

First stop is the lungs, where the blood picks up oxygen.
From there it's channelled all around your body through arteries
which branch at the ends to form capillary networks within
your body. This way, oxygen and nutrients are carried
to every cell in your body.

Waste is removed by capillaries too, as they link up to form
veins through which blood that needs oxygen is delivered
back to the heart. Each blood cell will go around this circuit
once a minute.

★ Insert your CD into your CD drive.
★ Pick your journey and follow the QTVR symbols.
★ Let the adventure begin!

# CIRCULATION
## Get your blood pumping!

The camera is positioned in three places: in the left ventricle of your heart, inside one of your blood vessels and inside one of your many capillaries. The CD takes you on the same journey as blood, starting in your heart. The following pages explain the vital parts and what is happening along the way.

WOW, this looks like a cave!

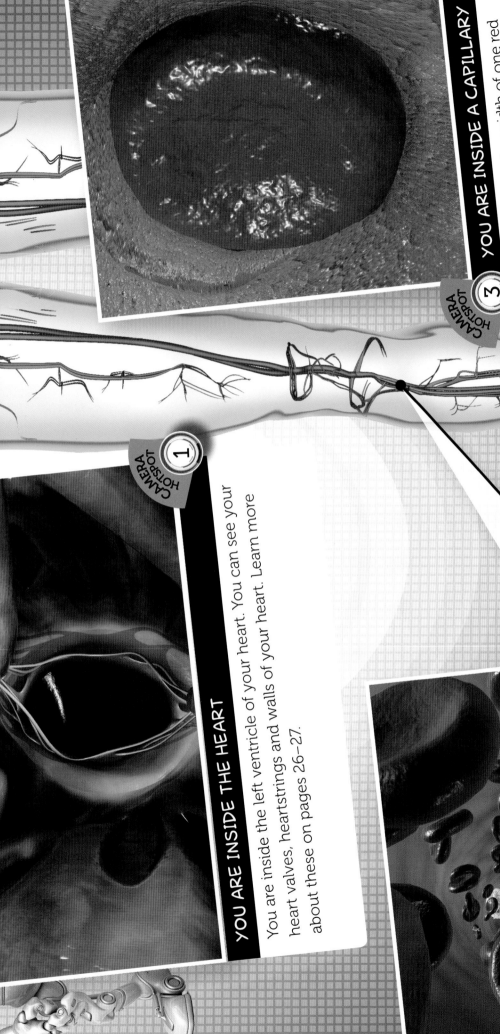

## YOU ARE INSIDE A CAPILLARY

This vessel is the width of one red blood cell. If you look closely you can see through its very thin wall. Learn more about this on page 28.

## YOU ARE INSIDE THE HEART

You are inside the left ventricle of your heart. You can see your heart valves, heartstrings and walls of your heart. Learn more about these on pages 26–27.

## YOU ARE INSIDE AN ARTERY

Look for three different types of cells – white blood cells, red blood cells and platelets. These are explained on page 29.

# Your heart

Your heart beats on average 60–80 times per minute when your body is resting, and about 2.5 billion times in your lifetime. It is so powerful that with each heartbeat it manages to pump blood around your entire body. Your heart never rests – if it did, you would die!

## AORTA

This is the largest artery in your body. From the left ventricle it carries oxygen-rich blood towards your body's tissues.

## SUPERIOR VENA CAVA

This vein carries oxygen-poor blood from your upper body into the right atrium.

## A hollow house

Your heart is hollow, so that blood can pass through it. It's also divided into different rooms like a house, with right and left sides which are both divided into an upper and a lower chamber. The upper chambers are known as the atria – the right atrium and left atrium. These are smaller than the lower chambers, known as the right ventricle and left ventricle. Blood comes in and out of your heart through blood vessels.

The beating of your heart can be felt in pulse points around your body. Can you find one?

## RIGHT ATRIUM

Oxygen-poor blood from the body enters your heart here and is then pumped into the right ventricle.

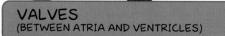

## What happens when my heart beats?

There are three stages of a heartbeat:

1. When your heart relaxes the right atrium fills with oxygen-poor blood from your body and the left atrium fills with oxygen-rich blood from your lungs. The semilunar valves close to prevent blood flowing backwards into the ventricles.

2. The left and right atria contract propelling blood through open valves into the left and right ventricles.

3. In the next phase of your heartbeat, the ventricles contract, the valves between the atria and ventricles close and blood is squeezed from your heart through open semilunar valves into the pulmonary vien, which carries blood to the lungs, and the aorta, which carries blood to the body.

## VALVES
### (BETWEEN ATRIA AND VENTRICLES)

This valve opens when the artrium contracts to push blood into the ventricle. It closes when the ventricle contracts to push blood out of the heart. This ensures that blood travels in one direction through the heart.

## INFERIOR VENA CAVA

This vein carries oxygen-poor blood from the abdomen and legs to the right atrium.

## 'Lub dub'

Every heartbeat produces two sounds, known as 'lub' and 'dub', that can be heard using a stethoscope. The longer, louder 'lub' sound is produced when the valves between the atria and ventricles close. The shorter, sharper 'dub' sound is produced when the semilunar valves close.

## PULMONARY ARTERY

This vessel's job is to carry oxygen-poor blood from the right ventricle to the lungs.

## PULMONARY VEIN

Once your blood is full of oxygen from the lungs it is carried to the left atrium along the pulmonary vein.

## SEMILUNAR VALVE

This valve stops blood flowing backwards when the ventricle relaxes.

## LEFT ATRIUM

Oxygen-rich blood carried from your lungs, enters the left atrium and is then pumped to the left ventricle.

## LEFT VENTRICLE

This pumps oxygen-rich blood out of your heart and into your aorta. The muscular wall of the left ventricle is thicker than that of the right ventricle. This gives it the power to push blood out of your heart with enough pressure to be able to flow around your body.

## HEART STRINGS

These fine cords stop the valve between the atrium and the ventricle turning inside out.

## PERICARDIUM

This double-layered bag encloses and protects your heart.

## CARDIAC MUSCLE

Only your heart has this amazing and unique type of muscle. It receives a greater supply of energy than any other muscle in your body, to ensure that the heart muscle fibres never get tired.

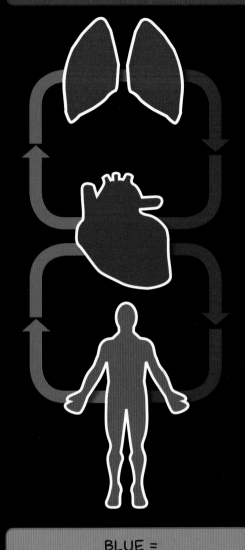

RED =
OXYGEN-RICH BLOOD

BLUE =
OXYGEN-POOR BLOOD

# A figure of eight

There are two loops within your circulatory system. One loop takes blood from your heart to your lungs to collect oxygen, then brings it back to your heart. This loop is called the pulmonary circulation.

The second loop is called the systemic circulation. It takes the oxygen-rich blood to your body's tissues, before returning to your heart to begin its journey along the first loop again ... and again and again!

# Your blood vessels

Did you know that just about every part of your body has blood vessels passing through it? The network of blood vessels that delivers blood around your body, together with blood and your heart, make up the circulatory system.

## Highways around your body

Your blood vessels make up a network of tubes that, if stretched out in a straight line, would encircle the planet two and a half times! They are busy one-way highways along which blood circulates around your entire body. There are three types of blood vessels in your body: arteries, veins and capillaries. All three have important jobs to do.

### HEART

This is your circulatory system's pump, providing the power to push blood along your arteries and back through your veins.

### INFERIOR VENA CAVA

Blood is carried from the lower part of your body to your heart by the inferior vena cava.

### COMMON ILIAC ARTERY

The common iliac artery supplies blood to your pelvis and legs.

### FEMORAL VEIN

Blood drains from the thigh towards your heart along this vein.

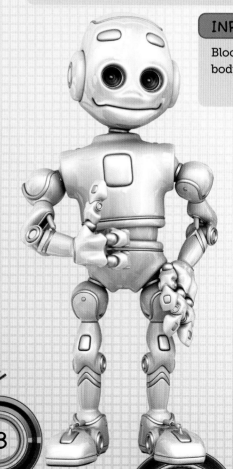

## COMMON CAROTID ARTERY

This supplies oxygen-rich blood to your head and brain.

## SUBCLAVIAN ARTERY

This supplies blood to your arm.

## SUBCLAVIAN VEIN

Oxygen-poor blood is carried from your arm towards your heart in this vein.

## BRACHIAL ARTERY

This branches from your subclavian artery to supply oxygenated blood to your upper arm.

## SUPERIOR VENA CAVA

Blood drains from the upper body to your heart along this major vein.

## DESCENDING AORTA

Blood travels to your abdomen and legs along this major artery.

## FEMORAL ARTERY

This is the main artery of the upper leg and supplies blood to your thigh and knee.

## ANTERIOR TIBIAL ARTERY

This artery supplies blood to your lower leg and foot.

## DORSALIS PEDIS ARTERY

Your ankle and the upper part of your foot receive their blood supply via this artery.

What are the differences between an artery, a vein and capillary?

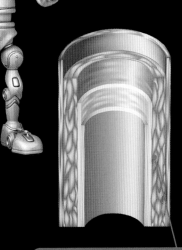

## Artery

Arteries carry oxygen-rich blood from your heart to all your body's tissues. They have thick, muscular walls to withstand the strong pressure of blood surging away from the heart. The walls of the artery expand with each pressure wave, and then bounce back as the wave subsides. You can feel this pulse whenever an artery is near the surface of the skin and passes over hard tissue, such as a bone in your wrist.

**ARTERY WALL**
It is made up of elastic tissue and muscle.

## Vein

Once your blood has delivered its oxygen and is laden with waste products from your body's cells, it is carried back to your heart along your veins. Veins have thinner walls than arteries because the pressure of the blood flow is no longer as high as it was in the arteries.

**VEIN VALVES**
These prevent the backflow of blood.

## Capillary

Tiny capillaries are the most abundant blood vessels in your body. Oxygen and nutrients pass through their thin walls to nourish your body's cells and tissues.

**CAPILLARY WALL**
This is just one cell thick.

# Your blood

Blood makes up almost one-tenth of your bodyweight, and it has many jobs. It's like your body's waiter, supplying each and every cell with the oxygen and nutrients it needs, and carrying away leftovers. Blood also acts like a soldier by helping to defend your body against invasion from bacteria and other germs. Its other job is to stop your body getting too hot or too cold.

## What is in your blood?

Blood is made up of various types of cells. Red blood cells carry oxygen so you need a lot of them, and they make up 44 per cent of your bloodstream. Equally important but less numerous are white blood cells, which defend your body against invaders such as germs. Platelets help blood to clot. Between them, white blood cells and platelets make up about one per cent of your blood. A fluid called plasma makes up the remaining 55 per cent. Thanks to plasma, blood is a liquid. Without it, your blood cells would not be able to circulate!

### RED BLOOD CELLS

Around 2 million red blood cells are produced every second by red bone marrow, to replace the same number of worn-out red blood cells, which are broken down and recycled by the spleen and liver. There are 25 trillion blood cells in your blood. The dimpled shape of red blood cells makes it easier for them to pick up oxygen.

I'm a red blood cell and there are 2.5 million of me in one pinhead-size drop of blood

I'm a platelet and there are 160,000 of me in one pinhead-size drop of blood.

I'm a white blood cell and there are 3,750 of me in one pinhead-size drop of blood.

### WHITE BLOOD CELLS

White blood cells are soldiers, defending you against germs that want to invade your body's tissues. They travel around the body to search out invaders.

## Why is my blood red?

Red blood cells get their colour from a protein called haemoglobin, which binds oxygen molecules so they can be transported around.

## The body's waiter

As well as oxygen, blood carries nutrients such as glucose, amino acids and fatty acids, which it picks up either from digested food or the stores of nutrients that the body keeps in the liver. As your body's cells take in these useful things, the blood collects waste products such as carbon dioxide. Carbon dioxide passes from tissue cells into the blood and is carried to the lungs to be breathed out.

## Temperature control

Blood helps maintain your body temperature at 37°C (98.6°F) by absorbing heat from warmer parts, such as the liver, muscles and heart, and carrying it to the cooler parts. Which part of your body gets coldest in winter? It's probably your nose, fingers or toes, all of which stick out so that the blood passing through them loses its heat quickly!

> I need a plaster!

When you cut yourself and a blood vessel is damaged blood leaks out of it.

Blood has the amazing ability to plug the cut by becoming gooey and caking together into a jelly-like mass – a clot that seals the area. Platelets become sticky soon after the damage takes place and clump together to plug the area. Also, white blood cells move in to track and destroy germs that have invaded from outside the body.

Then, a substance called fibrinogen is changed by a chemical reaction into a substance known as fibrin, which creates a kind of natural gauze over the cut. Red and white blood cells and platelets become caught up in the gauze to help form the clot – a kind of natural bandage.

### PLATELETS

These play a crucial role in clotting. They stop your blood from leaking out of your body if you are injured.

## What is sound?

**When something moves — whether it is a tiny pin dropping or a huge plane taking off — it creates sound waves.**

Your outer ear collects sound waves, which are vibrations in the air. Your middle ear passes these vibrations along tiny bones to the inner ear.

Your inner ear changes them into vibrations in fluid, and then into electrical nerve signals. Your middle and inner ears are protected from knocks by skull bones. The hairs and waxy lining of the outer ear canal gather and remove dust and germs.

★ Insert the CD into your CD drive.
★ Pick your journey and follow the QTVR symbols.
★ Let the adventure begin!

# HEARING
## Come hear and explore!

JOURNEY
4

CAMERA HOTSPOT

1   YOU ARE IN THE EAR CANAL

If you look through the hairs you can see the outside world beyond your ear flap. If you look the other way you can see your eardrum. Learn more about this on page 36.

Wow! I can see outside from here.

The camera is positioned in three places: in your ear canal, inside your middle ear and inside your cochlea. The CD takes you on the same route as sound. The following pages explain the vital parts and what is happening along the way.

CAMERA HOTSPOT

## 2 YOU ARE IN THE MIDDLE EAR

You can see the ossicles which are the smallest bones in your body. Learn more about these on page 37.

CAMERA HOTSPOT

## 3 YOU ARE INSIDE THE COCHLEA

This is a spiral-shaped fluid-filled chamber in the inner ear. Find out what happens in here on page 37.

# How we hear sounds

We cannot see sound waves in the air, but your ears can detect and transform them into electrical signals. When your brain interprets these signals you are able to hear many different sounds and noises.

## Your outer ear

Your ears might stick out and look odd, but there's a good reason for this. They are excellently well-adapted for funnelling sound waves into the ear canal.

Sound waves travel along the ear canal until they hit the eardrum, a thin sheet of membrane that is stretched across the ear canal. The mechanism really is similar to a musical drum, hence its name.

## Your middle ear

In your middle ear there are three tiny bones called the ossicles. These are attached to the ear drum at one end and the oval window at the other.

## Your inner ear

On the other side of the oval window is the cochlea. This is the part of the ear that turns the sound waves into electrical signals. It is a tiny fluid-filled tube coiled in a tall spiral like a snail's shell. Near the cochlea are more fluid-filled tubes – the semicircular canals. These help with balance. Without them, you'd fall over!

**EAR FLAP**

Also known as the pinna, this is the only visible part of your ear. Its funnel shape directs sound waves into your ear.

**EAR CANAL**

This is about half as long as your little finger. Sound waves travel along the ear canal until they hit the eardrum, which is at the far end of the ear canal. Ear wax and the hairs in the ear canal filter any dust or germs that travel into the ear.

**EARDRUM**

Located at the end of the ear canal, the eardrum marks the boundary between the outer and middle ear. When sound waves hit your eardrum, they cause this tightly stretched membrane to vibrate.

**SKULL BONES**

These protect the middle and inner ears from the effects of knocks and blows.

## OSSICLES

These three tiny linked bones carry the vibrations from the eardrum across the middle ear towards the inner ear.

## SEMICIRCULAR CANALS

These tiny tubes help you to keep your balance.

## OVAL WINDOW

This stirrup is attached to the oval window which is the intersection between the middle and inner ear.

## COCHLEA

The cochlea is filled with fluid. Movements of the oval window make waves in this fluid, which cause the micro-hairs set into the lining of the cochlea to move about. This makes the cells attached to these hairs create electrical signals that they send to the brain along the cochlear nerve.

## EUSTACHIAN TUBE

This tube is responsible for balancing air pressure in the middle ear.

## THE SMALLEST BONES IN YOUR BODY

The ossicles are a chain of bones. They are the smallest bones in your entire body. Their names reflect their shapes. The hammer is attached to the eardrum. Connected to the hammer on its other side is the anvil, which, in turn, is connected to the stirrup. The stirrup is attached on its other side to the oval window. When the eardrum vibrates, it causes the ossicles to move back and forth like a piston. This pulls and pushes the oval window, setting up vibrations in the fluid filling the inner ear.

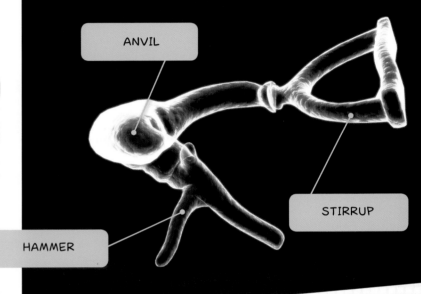

ANVIL

STIRRUP

HAMMER

## COCHLEAR NERVE

Connected to the cochlea, this is the nerve along which all the electrical signals created by the micro-hairs in the cochlea are sent to the brain for processing. The cochlea is filled with fluid. Movements of the oval window make waves in this fluid, which cause the micro-hairs set into the lining of the cochlea to move about. In response to this stimulation, these hairs create electrical signals that they send to your brain along the auditory nerve.

## Why do some people wear hearing aids?

Some people suffer from hearing loss. In most cases this happens because the cochlea cannot detect sounds properly. The remedy can be a tiny hearing aid attached to the ear flap. It has a microphone that picks up sounds, an amplifier that makes sounds louder, and a speaker that sends these louder sounds along the ear canal towards the cochlea.

# How do we balance?

You probably don't think much about how you stay upright, except for when you are about to fall over! But your ears, along with other senses, are working all the time to make sure you keep your balance.

## What keeps us upright?

Inside your inner ear, next to the cochlea, is a set of organs that make up the vestibular system. This system helps you balance and stay upright by detecting your head's movements and position. The balance organs send signals to your brain so it can monitor and control your body's movements and position – whether you are in a car, standing still, in a lift, doing a somersault or walking along a narrow wall.

## Your position and movement

There are two sets of fluid-filled balance organs in your inner ear: the semicircular canals and the utricle and saccule. Each one contains a chamber called the ampulla which has a jelly-like cap that sits over a set of hair cells. The hair cells pick up rotational movement so when you do a somersault your brain tells you what is happening. The utricle and saccule each have a jelly-like macula that contains hair cells. These detect the position of your head when you are not moving and also linear (straight-line) speeding up and slowing down movements, such as when a lift accelerates upwards or a car brakes and slows down.

### Teamwork

Your brain also uses information from other senses to help you keep your balance. Your eyes and feet tell your brain which way is up and which is down. If you blindfold yourself and take one foot off the ground, you'll find it much harder to keep your balance, as your brain is receiving no information from your eyes, and information only from one foot.

### VESTIBULAR NERVE

A nerve is attached to the ampulla in each semicircular canal. The electrical signals generated by the micro-hairs of the ampulla travel along this to your brain.

ANTERIOR
SEMICIRCULAR CANAL

POSTERIOR
SEMICIRCULAR CANAL

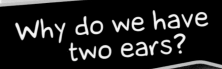

Having two ears helps your brain to work out where a sound is coming from. Depending on where the sound's source is located, sound waves arrive at one ear a fraction of a second before the other. Your brain uses this tiny time difference to pinpoint the source. Some animals can move their ear flaps to make direction finding even more accurate.

LATERAL
SEMICIRCULAR CANAL

## AMPULLA

Movement-detecting micro-hairs are embedded in this collection of minerals, found in each of the semicircular canals.

## UTRICLE

This detects the position of your head.

## SACCULE

Along with the utricle, the saccule detects the position of the head. It also detects how fast your head is moving, so if you are running, the saccule will let your brain know how fast you are going, and when you are speeding up or slowing down.

# JOURNEY
# 5

## NEW LIFE
### and the journey of a baby!

# Where does life begin?

**People say that your whole life is a journey – and it starts with one too.**

Beginning inside the uterus of a mother-to-be, a new life goes on an amazing nine-month-long voyage of transformation before it is ready to be born as a baby boy or girl.

★ Insert your CD into your CD drive.
★ Pick your journey and follow the QTVR symbols.
★ Let the adventure begin.

# NEW LIFE
## How does a baby form?

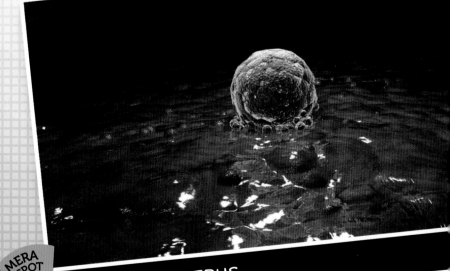

CAMERA HOTSPOT

1 INSIDE THE FALLOPIAN TUBE

You are in the fallopian tube and you can see an egg having been released from the ovary and waiting to be fertilised. Learn more about this on pages 44–45.

The camera is positioned in four places: inside the fallopian tube showing an egg waiting to be fertilised, inside a uterus (womb) showing a fertilised egg implanting into the lining of the uterus, inside a uterus showing a 12-week-old foetus and inside a uterus showing an 8-month-old foetus. The CD takes you on the same journey as a growing baby. The following pages explain the vital parts and what is happening along the way.

CAMERA HOTSPOT

2 INSIDE THE UTERUS

Here you can see a blastocyst implanting into the lining of the uterus. Why and how this happens is explained on page 46.

CAMERA
HOTSPOT
3

## INSIDE THE UTERUS – A 12-WEEK-OLD FOETUS

Here you can see what a 12-week-old foetus looks like. What is developing and how it is nourished is explained on page 47.

CAMERA
HOTSPOT
4

## INSIDE THE UTERUS – AN 8-MONTH-OLD FOETUS

You can see what an 8-month-old foetus looks like. How it has grown and developed since it was 12 weeks is explained on page 47.

# How does life begin?

Have you ever wondered how humans are made? It's amazing to think that every person in the world started out from just two cells – an egg cell from their mother and a sperm cell from their father. When the two cells fuse together in a process called fertilisation, a new life begins.

## Creating a new person

An egg and a sperm need to fuse together in order to create a new person. But sperm face some serious competition – thousands of them swim up along each fallopian tube looking for a single egg.

Those that reach the egg will try to burrow into it, but only one will succeed in breaking through the outer surface. The winning sperm leaves its tail at the entrance of the burrow and makes its way to the centre (nucleus) of the egg cell.

Once the egg nucleus and the sperm head fuse, a new person begins to form. You, your parents and even your school biology teacher all began life this way!

### EGG

The egg floats along the fallopian tube to the uterus. On its way, it may meet many sperm, one of which could fertilise it.

## What's the difference between an egg and a sperm?

### EGG NUCLEUS

Half of the genetic material required to make a new person is contained in the nucleus. The other half is in the head of the sperm.

### EGG

The egg cell, also known as the ovum, is the largest cell in the body, and the only human cell that can be seen without a microscope. It is about 0.12mm across – about the size of a small pin head. In its centre is the nucleus, which contains genetic information from the mother. This is surrounded by a strong membrane that the sperm must break through to reach it.

### SPERM

This expert swimmer has a head, which contains genetic information from the father, a middle piece that contains the fuel for the sperm's marathon swim, and a tail that lashes to and fro, propelling it forwards on its quest to find an egg to fertilise. You would need a powerful microscope to see a sperm as it is 0.05mm long.

## CUMULUS

These are also known as cloud cells. They protect the egg until it comes into contact with the sperm and they tell the sperm that this egg is ready to be fertilised.

## What are genes?

Each cell in your body contains genes, which are the instructions needed to build, maintain and repair that cell. Genes determine your shape and physical appearance and are inherited from your parents, so if they are both tall with brown eyes you probably will be too.

Genes are contained in chromosomes, which are made up of a long molecule called DNA. Each egg and sperm cell carries 23 chromosomes, and when the two fuse at fertilisation the combined set of 46 chromosomes contains all the information needed for building a new person.

## Boy or girl?

Why does a new person become a boy or a girl? This depends on which sperm cell manages to fertilise the egg.

There is a chromosome in both the egg cell and sperm cell that is responsible for determining sex. In the egg cell, this is always an X chromosome, but the sperm cell can contain either an X or a Y chromosome. So the person ends up with either XX or XY as their 'chromosome pair'. XX makes them a girl, while XY makes them a boy.

A new person's sex is all down to which sperm swam the fastest to their mother's egg!

## FALLOPIAN TUBE

The fallopian tube is lined with folded, moist, mucus membrane that contains two types of cells: cells that exude mucus which protects the lining of the tubes and ciliated cells which are covered with hair-like structures known as cilia. These beat in a wave-like motion to move the egg along the fallopian tube towards the uterus.

# What happens inside?

How does a fertilised egg become a human being? An amazing amount of development takes place inside your mother's body during the nine months between fertilisation and birth. In this time, the single cell is transformed into a fully functioning person.

## A baby in the making

Once it has been fertilised, the single-cell egg floats along the fallopian tube on its way to the uterus. Meanwhile, it divides into two cells, then each of those two cells does the same thing. And so on, again and again!

The genetic instructions contained in each of the newly-made cells guide how they will each develop to make all the body parts of a new person. As cell division continues, an inner and outer group of cells develop. The inner group of cells will develop into an embryo, and the outer group of cells will feed the embryo until it can get nourishment from the mother's body.

### 16-CELL STAGE

After fertilisation, the egg divides into two cells, and both of these split into two. This process continues until, 72 hours after fertilisation, there are 16 cells clumped together in a ball, looking a bit like a blackberry.

## Implantation and growth

About five or six days after fertilisation, the bundle of cells, called a blastocyst, has reached the end of the fallopian tube and enters the uterus, where it embeds itself into the thick, blood-rich uterus lining. Cell division continues and, as cells multiply, different types of cells (such as blood cells, muscle cells, nerve cells and so on) move around the tiny body to take their correct places and begin to develop into the various organs, muscles and bones.

The most dramatic development takes place in the first two months after fertilisation, after which the developing baby looks quite human, although it is still very tiny. From then until birth, it will grow enormously, which can be seen on the outside by how big the mother's tummy becomes.

## How is a growing baby fed?

How does a tiny foetus get the nourishment it needs in order to develop? Once the blastocyst has embedded in the lining of the uterus, its inner part develops into an embryo. Its outer part digests lining cells to release the food that feeds the embryo. By the second month after fertilisation a placenta has developed. This transfers food and oxygen from the mother's blood supply to the embryo through the umbilical cord.

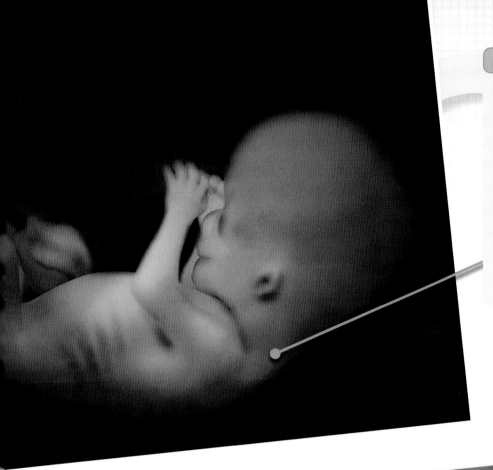

## 12-WEEK-OLD FOETUS

At 12 weeks after fertilisation the tiny fertilised egg has been transformed into a tiny baby-to-be, or foetus, made from billions of cells. By this stage the foetus looks human, with clear facial features and forward-facing eyes. It is about the size of a lemon. Her or his internal organs are now in place, and the heart is beating and pumping blood. The limbs are in proportion to the rest of the body, but the head is large by comparison. The foetus's fingers and toes are now separate and have nails.

## 8-MONTH-OLD FOETUS

Now just a few weeks from being born, the foetus is approaching full development although the brain is still growing quickly. In these final weeks, fat is laid down under the skin to provide the baby, when it is born, with energy and insulation to keep it warm. The foetus can hear sounds from inside or outside its mother's body, its eyes blink and respond to light, and it follows patterns of sleeping and waking. Its movements can be felt by its mother. As during most of pregnancy, the foetus receives food and oxygen from its mother through the umbilical cord and placenta.

47

# PICTURE CREDITS

The publishers would like to thank the following sources for their kind permission to reproduce the pictures in this book.

Key. T: Top, B: bottom, L: Left, R: Right, C: Centre

© **Carlton Books:** 2-3c, 5, 8, 10r, 11, 12-13c, 13b, 17, 18-19c, 19r, 19br, 21, 24-25, 28-29c, 34c, 36-37c, 44b, 48-49c, /Ceri Hurst: 1b, 2l, 48-49 (5 diagrams)
**DK Images:** 20bl, 20br, 21tr, 29c, 39
**iStockphoto.com:** 1t, 2b, 4b, 7, 8r, 10b, 11r, 12l, 15tl, 18bl, 19tr, 20l, 20tr, 23l, 24, 26l, 28l, 29c, 30b, 31c, 32tl, 34-35c, 37br, 38c, 39tr, 40l, 44c, 45tl, 45r
**Science Photo Library:** 26-27c, 37r, 46r, 47bl
**Thinkstockphotos.com:** 30bl